The Sumerians

THE
SUMERIANS

BY LEILA MERRELL FOSTER

Franklin Watts
New York London Toronto Sydney
A First Book 1990

Cover photograph courtesy of: Scala/Art Resource, NY

Photographs courtesy of: The Oriental Institute, University of Chicago:
pp. 2, 29, 30 top, 34 bottom, 40 top, 45, 47, 51, 54, 55; The University
of Michigan, Department of Near Eastern Studies: p. 10 (G.G. Cameron);
Culver Pictures Inc.: p. 13; UPI/Bettmann Newsphotos: p. 15;
Scala/Art Resource, NY: p. 19 left; Lee Boltin Picture Library:
pp. 19 right, 24 top; The University Museum, University of Pennsylvania:
pp. 21, 22, 23, 36, 40 bottom; The Metropolitan Museum of Art:
pp. 24 bottom (The Dodge Fund), 34 top (The Harris Brisbane Dick Fund);
Historical Pictures Service, Chicago: p. 30 bottom; The Bettmann Archive; p. 42.

Library of Congress Cataloging-in-Publication Data
Foster, Leila Merrell.
The Sumerians / by Leila Merrell Foster.
p.   cm.—(A First book)
Includes bibliographical references.
Summary: Looks at arts and sciences of ancient Sumeria, its
religious customs, and the effect it left on the Western world,
describing how archaeologists discovered this lost civilization.
ISBN 0-531-10874-0
1. Sumerians—Juvenile literature. [1. Sumerians.] I. Title.
II. Series.
DS72.F67 1990
935'.01—dc20   90-12132   CIP   AC

To my mother and father,
Leila Virginia Merrell Foster
and
George Henry Foster

Contents

The Discovery of the Sumerians 11

The Rise and Fall of
the Sumerian Civilization 27

Life in the Sumerian City-State 38

The Legacy of the Sumerians 53

Glossary 57

For Further Reading 60

Index 61

The Sumerians

*Darius had his achievements inscribed in
three languages on the Behistun rock.*

The Discovery of
the Sumerians

THE YOUNG BOY climbed out over the carvings on a monument 500 feet high up on a Persian cliff in Western Asia. Using the slight indentations in the rock as hand- and footholds, he made his way twenty feet across the steep, almost smooth face to the other side of the carving. Then he rigged a rope so that he could make his paper tracing of the strange writing on this expanse of stone for the Englishman waiting below.

The local men who tracked mountain goats in the area said that no one could do what the boy was attempting. Yet the boy, who was from the Kurdish people and came from a distance away, had volunteered to try. He had climbed up a *cleft* in the rock.

When he was high enough, he drove in a peg to which he attached the rope. After risking his neck by crossing the face of the monument, he fixed another peg to which he tied the end of the rope. Then, by attaching a small ladder, he made himself a swinging seat from which he was able to make the paper tracing that the Englishman would take home.

This happened in 1846. The Englishman, Sir Henry Creswicke Rawlinson, was convinced that this monument—which contained the same inscription in three different languages—would be the key to breaking the code of the still puzzling language written in a strange script called *cuneiform*. Rawlinson had used a telescope and had climbed as far as he could on the cliff face to copy the inscriptions in the first two languages. It was the third language, which proved to be Babylonian, that was the prize. Little did the Persian emperor, Darius I, who ordered this monument carved on the Behistun rock high above the plain in 516 B.C., suspect that the boast of his achievements would help later scholars learn of civilizations more ancient than his.

Translating from the ancient languages that they knew, the scholars, with the help of inscriptions like the one found on the Behistun rock, were able to begin to read Babylonian and Assyrian. The

*Sir Henry Creswicke Rawlinson was determined
to decipher ancient languages.*

cuneiform script was used for several ancient languages—just as the letters on this page can be used for English, French, and Spanish, but not for Arabic and Chinese. Yet one scholar, Edward Hincks, suspected that the Babylonians had not invented the cuneiform script. The Babylonians wrote with characters that stood for syllables, and the cuneiform looked as though it had been developed by people who had not always used syllables.

While the world before the nineteenth century knew of great empires like the Egyptians, the Babylonians, and the Assyrians, it did not know of the existence of the Sumerians—a people who lived 5,000 to 6,000 years ago in the southern part of the Tigris and Euphrates river plains located in what is now the country of Iraq. Other ancient peoples had left behind impressive stone monuments, temples, and palaces, or had been written about by name in books of ancient history. But the Sumerians had to be rediscovered through their writings, which had been copied by other civilizations, and through excavations of the buried cities they left behind.

These cities had been constructed largely with mud bricks made with clay from the banks of the two great rivers. Unlike stone, mud bricks fall apart in a heavy rain or flood and must be rebuilt. New

During this excavation in a corner of Nippur, Iraq, archaeologists unearthed clay tablets inscribed by Sumerians.

layers were added each century, and quite a mound accumulated until the city was abandoned for a new site. These mounds are called *tells*. Archaeologists, scientists who excavate and study these tells, began to tackle the sites of several ancient cities. They found remains of what is now considered to be the oldest human civilization—the Sumerian.

While the hot and damp climate of the area had destroyed many artifacts of Sumerian life, one spectacular excavation has revealed pieces of sculpture, musical instruments, helmets, and crowns. In 1922, archaeologist Sir Leonard Woolley led the group who discovered these items in the tombs of some important persons who had lived in the city of Ur.

It would be hard to guess from the location of Ur (in what is now southern Iraq) that the place had once been a great city. The Euphrates River, which once ran through the city, is today twelve miles away in a new riverbed. A change in the color of the sand marking the banks of the old river bed and its irrigation canals can be seen from an airplane. Around 2000 B.C., when the great temple that is now in ruins was new, the city covered about four square miles and was home to 500,000 people. Perhaps with the shift in the course of the river and a change in the climate, the city could no longer grow food and was abandoned.

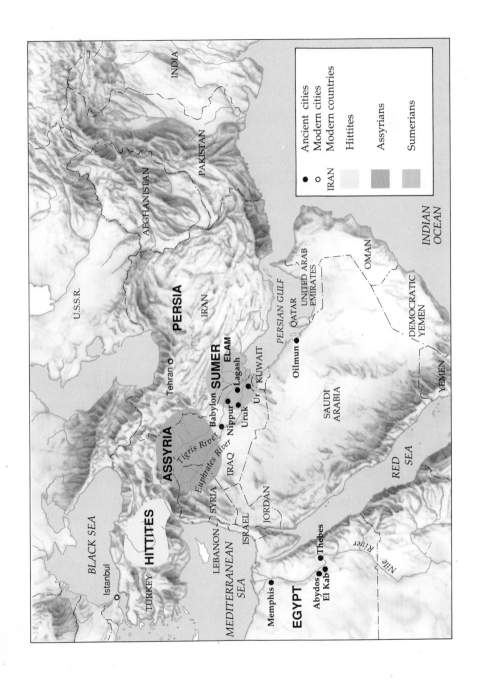

Ancient cities ●
Modern cities ○
Modern countries IRAN

Hittites
Assyrians
Sumerians

INDIA

PAKISTAN

AFGHANISTAN

U.S.S.R.

PERSIA

IRAN

OMAN

INDIAN
OCEAN

UNITED ARAB
EMIRATES

QATAR

PERSIAN GULF

Dilmun ●

DEMOCRATIC
YEMEN

YEMEN

SAUDI
ARABIA

RED
SEA

Tehran ○

SUMER

ELAM

Babylon ●
Lagash ●

Nippur ●
Uruk ●

Ur ● KUWAIT

Tigris River

Euphrates River

IRAQ

ASSYRIA

JORDAN

SYRIA

ISRAEL

LEBANON

BLACK SEA

TURKEY

Istanbul ○

HITTITES

MEDITERRANEAN
SEA

Memphis ●

EGYPT

Abydos ●
El Kab ●

Thebes ●

Nile River

Two very skilled persons worked on the team of archaeologists at Ur. Woolley was very successful in choosing good places to dig to try to find the remains of the Sumerians. When he was on the location of a dig, he was up at sunrise and would often work until two or three the next morning making lists of items found or studying the work. In charge of the diggers was an Arab named Shaikh Hamoudi ibn Ibrahim. Hamoudi had a boatman chant a song while he used his spade as though he were pulling a boat through water. The other workers would join in the chorus, and it made the work easier and more enjoyable.

During the 1926–1927 season of digging, the team uncovered many graves that provided clues to the dates when people were buried. Only one grave of an important person was discovered. On the last day the most valuable item, a gold dagger, was found. The workers had to leave, but the local chief who lived in the area gave his word that no one would touch the site. No one did. The next year, the team uncovered wonderful objects of art such as the Sumerian Standard (panels showing scenes of life in peace and war), a gold helmet, gold vases, and a headdress or crown.

Woolley also discovered a pit that had a limestone floor. Because most Sumerian buildings were

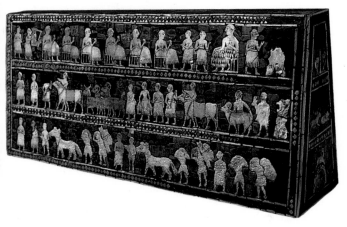

A gold dagger in a grave indicated the burial of an important person. (Below) The Sumerian Standard was a doubly valuable find: not only is it a beautifully preserved piece of art, but its pictures depict scenes from Sumerian life.

made of mud bricks, and the nearest limestone was some thirty miles away, this find was unusual. Woolley guessed that the limestone floor might actually be the roof of a royal tomb. He dug down and discovered rooms that had once been covered with a stone dome. The tombs were empty because robbers in earlier times had found them and stolen the contents.

Then, in a nearby room, the diggers came upon some skeletons. There were five bodies lying side by side on top of a mat. Under the mat lay the carefully arranged bodies of ten women. The women had been wearing headdresses of gold, lapis lazuli (a blue stone), and carnelian (a red stone). At the end of the row lay the remains of a harp which had been decorated with a gold head of a bull. Also near the remains was a gold-decorated wood *sledge chariot* and the bones of animals that had drawn it. Examination of the bones revealed that they were oxen. Skeletons of the men who handled the animals were close at hand. A beautiful statuette of a ram caught in a thicket may have been the stand for a plate of offerings. However, no one body seemed to have been given special treatment, and the empty room at the end of the pit probably meant that the royal tomb had been robbed long ago.

Still another pit filled with bodies was discovered. Six soldiers with copper spears were laid out in orderly rows. Court ladies with gold and silver headdresses and silver headbands to keep their hair in place were discovered. A silver disc was found near one of the ladies. Woolley wondered what it was until he realized that it was one of the headbands rolled up. Apparently one of the ladies had forgotten to put it on for her funeral. Many cups

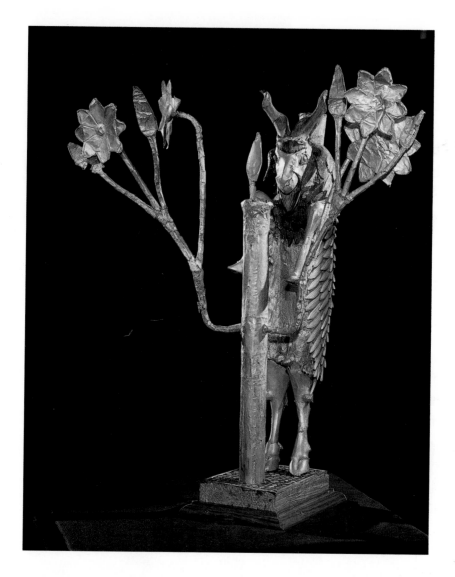

This sculpture of a ram, made of gold and lapis around 2600 B.C., shows the artistry and craftsmanship of the Sumerians.

This gold cup and poplar-leaf necklace shine on—even though they were made over four thousand years ago!

These discoveries are something of a mystery. No other mass burials of so many persons have been found among the Sumerians. The myths and stories do not contain any idea of people being buried along with the ruler—with one exception. A story about the death of a legendary Sumerian king named Gilgamesh tells of members of his court going with him to his grave. Gilgamesh was special because he was to be god of the underworld, so perhaps his court had to go with him. The persons in the tombs also may have represented gods and goddesses and so took their followers with them. Still, because there are not more stories about such events, the burial of so many people on the death of the ruler may not have been a common practice.

Woolley kept on digging to establish the age of the tombs. Only three feet farther down, the diggers came upon mud that contained nothing indicating that humans had ever lived there. After eight feet of this mud without one human item, they came upon some broken pots from a period of about 5000 B.C., and below that were reed huts of people who had lived there before. People still use reeds for their houses in the delta area of the rivers. Why the eight feet of mud without any human implement? Perhaps there was a great flood in that area that made it uninhabitable. In other places in Iraq there are signs of several floods at different periods—not just one big one. But at some time there must have been a large flood that gave rise to the story of the Sumerian gods telling a man to build an ark to save himself and his family.

What the tombs of Ur tell us is that the Sumerians were very skillful in creating the golden objects that survived. They must have encouraged artists and loved beauty. The harps tell us that they must have loved music. By living together in cities and by developing their talents, the Sumerians had created a great civilization.

There are many other tells, mounds likely to have been ancient cities, remaining to be excavated by archaeologists. New discoveries may give us a clearer picture of the life of the Sumerians.

The Rise and Fall of
the Sumerian Civilization

How DID THIS first great civilization come to exist?
At least four periods have been identified when gla-
ciers covered the land. The last period is dated at
about 120,000 years ago and ended about 20,000
B.C. Humans existed during this period. They lived
in the open or in caves, and hunted and gathered
wild fruit and roots. The Shanidar Cave in the north
of Iraq and other areas give us hints of what life was
like in these early times.

About 9,000 years ago, humans learned how to
tame animals and how to plant crops rather than
just gather food. Now they were able to settle down
in one place to live. They learned how to make
shelters out of clay in areas where there was not

much wood or stone. Stone bowls, reed baskets, animal skins, and gourds used as containers were replaced by baked clay dishes. It was discovered that metal could be manufactured to replace stone implements.

As several families began to live together, they had to learn how to govern themselves. Perhaps as the climate changed and turned drier, people were forced to gather along the two great rivers, the Tigris and the Euphrates.

Sometime around 3500 and 3000 B.C., cities were formed. These communities were actually city-states as there was no government linking the cities, which often fought each other over claims to territory and water. As people gathered in one place and shared ideas, there was an explosion of inventions.

Spring floods deposited silt on the delta between the two great rivers, creating rich farm land. In order to keep plants alive during the summer heat, farmers learned to supply their fields with water through the use of irrigation ditches. They developed plows and used their oxen to pull the plows in their fields. They poured seeds with a funnel attached to the wood or metal plow and invented the planter. They developed tools to measure their fields and water systems. Planting and harvesting

*The Sumerians hitched animals to vehicles
with wheels for transportation.*

The Sumerians could tell a good fish story. They enjoyed their banquets.

Below: A spokeless wheel that was found in Ur.

are done best if the farmer has some kind of calendar. The Sumerians developed one based on the phases of the moon.

The Sumerians also invented the wheel for making pottery and for transportation. The first wheels were solid— without any spokes. Some scientists think that the potter's wheel came first and was tipped on end to make a wheel for carts. The Sumerians put sails on boats so that they could travel longer distances to trade with others for the metals they needed.

— Because their farming methods were so efficient, not everyone had to work at producing food. Specialization of labor was possible. Some were skilled at making pots, weaving, or metalworking. Others became priests and priestesses devoted to looking after the gods and goddesses the people worshiped. Rulers, fighters, and storytellers were able to concentrate their time and effort on their specialized tasks.

Writing and mathematics were developed. Over 5,000 years ago, people existed without numbers or the written word. If farmers wanted to know how many oxen and bushels of grain were available for trade, they had to count them. If they had five oxen and five bushels of grain, they might not make the connection that the idea of five could be applied to both oxen and grain. In order to avoid going outside to count the oxen each time, someone may have had the idea to make five small clay figures of oxen that could be kept inside a home. Here was the beginning of a representation or token of a larger thing. Then someone may have looked at the five tokens for oxen and the five tokens of a different shape for jars of grain and realized that the idea of five could be applied to anything, not just specifically to oxen and grain.

Archaeologists have discovered collections of these tokens. At first they did not know what they had found. Were the flat ones lids to jars? Were the round ones parts of a game belonging to some of the game boards that had been discovered? Some tokens looked like a very small model of an animal. Some had strange markings on them.

If farmers wanted to store their grain together with that of their neighbors, they would have to know how much grain they had put in the storage space. They could make a token out of clay to represent their share. They might make a larger token to stand for a larger amount.

If they wanted to ship grain to someone else and wanted to let the other person know how much was sent, they could make a clay envelope for the tokens. On the outside they could stamp the shape of the token and a figure to show how many tokens were on the inside. The token shape could then become a written word and the figure a number.

As people had to keep track of lots of things—pottery, wool, fish, dates, bread—tokens of many shapes would have to be developed and remembered. Yet some ideas were not so easily pictured. How could the idea of "stand" or "go" be portrayed?

Someone thought up the idea of using the symbol for "foot" for all three ideas—stand, go, and foot—and letting people decide on the meaning by how it was used. Writing became even easier when another person had the idea of using picture signs for the sounds of the spoken word. Now anything could be described with about 600 signs, which was a third of the number of picture symbols that were needed before.

As this system of writing was developed, no longer were the tools simply tokens in clay envelopes. Clay tablets were used on which marks could be made with reeds cut from the plentiful supply along the riverbanks. It is hard to make curving lines with these tools. Therefore, the picture signs were simplified into wedge-shaped marks. (The name "cuneiform" given to the Sumerian writing is Latin for "wedge-shaped.") Because it is easier not to smudge the clay on the tablets if the writer goes from left to right in horizontal rows, writing came to be done this way instead of going up and down or from right to left. Cuneiform was used for the languages of many other nations. Its last use by a people was recorded in the first century A.D.

Not everyone could read and write. Scribes specialized in this task and set up schools to train others. The Sumerians began to write down long

*Cuneiform verses are
inscribed on the
lap of this statue,
which dates back to
2150 B.C.*

*The tablet below bears a
cuneiform
inscription
of part of the Epic
of Gilgamesh.*

stories, like the Epic of Gilgamesh, which is read even today. From simple numbers, the Sumerians mastered a mathematical system based on the number sixty. Sixty was good because it could be divided by twelve other numbers. It may have contributed to the development of the Arabic decimal system based on tens. Traces of the Sumerian idea are present in our sixty-minute hour and in a circle made up of 360 degrees. Writing and counting helped the Sumerians to share and to develop ideas. With these tools, the resources of the city could be divided up for different purposes.

The cities of Sumer grew in strength and size. People could be taxed to pay for the building of walls for fortification and the digging of better irrigation ditches for the crops. Wars between cities and clashes with foreign tribes were recorded in the stories of the Sumerians. Scholars are divided over whether the Sumerians were the first people in the territory or whether they were later settlers. Words have turned up from three different language groups which would indicate a mix of people at an early stage.

A war between two of the city-states, with the others taking sides, weakened the Sumerians. An outsider from another group of people, the Akkadians, was able to come in and conquer all the city-

*Mounds that rise from a flat plain
may indicate the remains of an
ancient city. This photograph shows the
excavation of the ancient city of Nippur.*

states. This man, Sargon the Great, who lived from around 2334 to 2279 B.C., was able to unite the cities into a nation and push its boundaries out to become a large empire. The Akkadian Empire did not last long, however. It collapsed when a palace revolution unseated the ruler around 2193 B.C. A period of lawlessness and new invasions followed. The Sumerian cities, influenced by the ideas and language of the Akkadians, continued to exist. Then the Elamites invaded Sumer. The city of Ur was sacked and burned around 2004 B.C.

Thus the Sumerian rule came to an end as other conquerors took over and new civilizations, such as the Babylonians and the Assyrians, emerged. Yet the newcomers borrowed much from Sumerian civilization and preserved it in their own libraries.

Life in the Sumerian
City-State

A CITY-STATE in Sumer consisted of the city itself, suburbs, nearby towns, and the gardens, palm groves, and grain fields surrounding them. One of the largest, Lagash, had 1,800 square miles of territory and a population of 30,000 to 35,000. The Sumerians may have had as many as fourteen major cities with other areas also subject to their influence. For their farming and trade communities to succeed, they needed a plentiful supply of water and enough peace to be able to carry on business. Too little or too much flooding of the rivers could mean hunger. Plagues of locusts could wipe out a crop. People had to fear snakes, scorpions, hyenas, lions, wild dogs, and wolves. And there was always the danger of attack from other cities or tribes of other peoples. Unlike the Egyptians, who lived in a territory less likely to be attacked by human or natural forces, the Sumerians tended to look at the dark side of life.

Religion was very important to the Sumerians. The city was owned and protected by a god or goddess, and the people were servants of that deity. The temple, the house of the god or goddess, was the largest building in the city. Like the homes of the people, the temple was built of mud brick. When it rained, some of the mud brick would be destroyed and have to be rebuilt. When the temple was repaired, it was often enlarged and made taller. Eventually, the temple became a tall building of several stories that towered over the flat landscape that surrounded it. These towers were called *ziggurats*. The ziggurat at Babylon, a city that was built some years after the Sumerians ruled, may have been the one remembered in the Biblical story of the Tower of Babel.

All life and nature was believed to be controlled by some 3,000 gods and goddesses. Some of these deities were more powerful than others. An was lord of the sky and had his main temple at Uruk. Although designated as the chief god, he did not seem to exercise as much power over human lives as

(Top) An artist's rendition shows a reconstruction of the Temple Oval and surrounding walls that were built around 2800 B.C. (Bottom) Time and the elements have worn down many of the temples and buildings from that era.

Enlil, lord of the air and patron god of the Nippur city-state. Enlil had separated the earth from the sky, thereby creating the world. He chose the rulers of Sumer and Akkad. Enki was lord of the earth and the fresh water of the rivers and wells. Dumuzi, also referred to as Tammuz, was a god associated with vegetation, flocks, and cattle. His wife, Inanna, goddess of love and procreation, was a powerful deity. The sacred marriage of Dumuzi and Inanna, reenacted by the king and a priestess, was a form of worship to ensure the productivity of the land and the people. The Sumerian deities were very much like humans: they ate, drank, fought, became angry, and fell in love.

The Sumerians believed that they had been created by the gods out of clay in order to be slaves. The deities would let the humans know when they needed bread and beer by making their wants known to the priests and priestesses in the temple. Sometimes the gods would communicate through omens such as the particular shape of the liver of a sheep that had been sacrificed to them.

The Sumerians did their best to keep on the good side of the gods and goddesses by making offerings and prayers. Each city had its special god or goddess who protected it. Each family had personal gods or goddesses who looked after the mem-

Here, the king of Ur pours out an offering to the moon god Nannar.

bers of the household. If something went wrong, the Sumerians assumed that they must have displeased their protector or that their protector had lost out in a fight with another god or goddess.

The priests and priestesses gained more power and controlled more land. They needed people who could do different kinds of work—leaders of worship, managers, artists, musicians, scribes, cooks, weavers, and field workers. These people, and the widows and orphans for whom the temples were responsible, had to be fed. We have a record that one of the temples around 3000 B.C. was giving bread and beer each day to 1,200 people. Bread and beer were everyday food, but on special feast days there would be meat, fish, dates, and other treats.

THE SUMERIANS had some of the same questions about life that we do. How were we created? Why do we get sick and have problems? What happens when we die? Many different ideas and stories were developed to try to answer these questions. One of the most famous of the stories is the Epic of Gilgamesh.

Gilgamesh was the king of the city-state of Uruk. He was told of an uncivilized man, Enkidu, who lived with the animals. The king sent a prostitute to tame Enkidu and teach him the ways of civilization. When Enkidu came to the city of Uruk, he first fought the king, but then became good friends with Gilgamesh. The two went off together to explore the world, but Enkidu angered the gods and fell sick with a long and painful disease. When Enkidu died, Gilgamesh felt great grief. He then decided to go in search of immortality.

Gilgamesh went for advice to Zi-u-sudra, who had survived a great flood by building a huge boat at the direction of the gods. (The story of Zi-u-sudra is similar in several ways to the story of Noah and the Ark found in the Bible.) Gilgamesh was told by Zi-u-sudra to obtain a plant that grew at the bottom of the ocean. Although Gilgamesh succeeded in getting the plant, it was stolen from him by a snake when he was asleep. Gilgamesh failed in his attempt to be immortal like the gods and had to die like humans do. The names of Zi-u-sudra and Gilgamesh are also found in ancient lists of Sumerian kings.

The Sumerians had some stories about what happens after death, but the stories appear to contradict each other. For the most part, they thought the afterlife would be bad. According to one view, however, persons living a good life did better after death than those who were wicked.

The ruler of the city-state was considered the

This statue of the king was found buried in the ground near the door of the temple he was responsible for building. The king carries on his head the clay or mortar for laying the first bricks of the new building.

"shepherd" of his people. He had been chosen by the gods and was responsible to the deities for the life of his people. One very important duty of the king was to go through a ritual on New Year's Day so that the people would be rich and the crops would be good. In a big festival, the king climbed to the top of the ziggurat to the room in which the fertility goddess Inanna lived. The king was married symbolically to a priestess representing the goddess. Inanna would then see that the king's city prospered.

In theory the city was owned by its main god or goddess. In practice the temple owned only some of the land, which it rented out. The rest was owned by citizens as their property. At first, the ruler was no more than a citizen pressed into service for a specific period of time or when there was a crisis. Decisions were reached in consultation with other citizens of the city. We have the record of one ruler who sought advice from an assembly of citizens that was divided into two groups or houses—the elders and the fighting men. When the ruler had to decide whether or not to go to war with another city, he went to the elders, who voted against the war. The ruler did not like that decision, so he went next to the assembly of the fighting men; they decided to go to war.

An image of a Sumerian boat is carved into a jar. Note that the man uses a pole to push the boat along.

Fighting between cities made war and defense important to the citizens. The power of the rulers increased. Eventually, the ruler became king for life and was allowed to decide who should get his power when he died. The wife of the king often had an important public role. We have the record of one who was the head of an important temple. The power of the rulers grew as more taxes were imposed to maintain the defenses of the city against hunting tribes and other cities. Tax collectors and scribes were necessary to manage the wealth the king controlled.

Several classes of people lived in the city-state. The nobles, who made up the assembly of elders, owned large amounts of land and controlled the temple land. Their farms were worked by slaves or farmers who had to share their crops with the owner. The commoners, who owned plots of land as family holdings, might farm their land or work in other trades. They were probably the ones who spoke in the assembly of fighting men. A third group consisted of people who did not own land but worked in the temple or the palace. They might be given temporary use of some land and were supplied with food and wool. Finally, there were the slaves. This group consisted of prisoners taken in war, freemen who were made slaves as punishment, children sold by parents who needed money, or persons who paid off a debt by agreeing that their family would be slaves for several years. Slaves were property. Punishment was severe if they tried to escape. An average price for an adult male was less than the price for a farm animal. However, slaves did have certain legal rights. They could carry on a business, and they could buy their freedom. Since it was to the advantage of the slave owner to keep slaves healthy, the slaves usually were treated well.

The need for defense and for irrigation ditches strengthened the king's power and was the chief reason for collecting taxes. Sometimes the power to tax was misused. One reform-minded king, Uruk-agina of Lagash, left records that he had limited the taxes and the power of the officials that collected them, that he had protected the poor, and that he had seen that justice was done.

The decisions of another king, Ur-Nammu, were collected. It is from the Sumerian city-state of Nippur that we have one of the earliest of these codes or collection of laws. Punishment could be cruel. A thief might be stoned to death with stones on which his crime was written. A woman who said something she should not (the tablet is not clear what) might have her teeth crushed with bricks on which her wrongdoing was written.

Family life in Sumer contained the same problems that still exist between husbands and wives and between children and parents. Records show that fathers were worried that their sons were wasting their lives and would not amount to anything. Mothers taught their daughters how to find a boyfriend. A friend advised a young woman not to marry a man who comes from the mountains. The match will not be good, she said, because the man lives in a tent, eats uncooked meat, is a fighter, and probably will not be buried when he dies. A father found his daughter-in-law hard to tolerate.

However, the ideal family life is one in which parents and children love each other. Brothers had an important duty toward the family if the father was unable to act. Widows and orphans were taken care of by the temples. Kinship ties were very important.

Children learned by watching others do tasks. Schools where children were taught to read and write were only for the privileged few who would become scribes. Scribes entered school when they were very young and they trained for many years. The school day lasted from sunrise to sunset. Beating with a stick was the punishment for talking out of turn, standing when you were not supposed to, or going outside the school gate. Copying clay tablets and reciting from them was the way the scribes were taught.

The clay tablets that have survived often contain lists of things showing that the Sumerians had begun to put things in groups and categories. Names of different kinds of fish would be on one

Sumerian women had pierced ears for earrings.

tablet while names of cities would be on another. The Sumerians were good observers of what went on around them. One clay tablet records a sighting of a bright star that suddenly appeared in 4000 B.C. Astronomers today confirm that there must have been a supernova about that time.

Scribes kept the records of the temples and palaces. They wrote business contracts for people. Since most people could not read or write, they would "sign" the contract by making their mark— rolling their cylinder seal across the clay tablet to indicate their approval. It is from the clay tablets and the designs on the cylinder seals that we have learned much about the lives of the Sumerians.

The Legacy of
the Sumerians

THAT YOU ARE reading the words on this page may be thanks to the Sumerians who developed writing. That you can make a shopping list may be thanks to the people who put tokens in clay envelopes and marked them with the beginning of written words and figures. That you know that 2 plus 2 equals 4 of anything is thanks to a Sumerian who first understood this possibility.

When you get into a car or bus, think of the person who first had the idea that a wheel could be used for transportation. When you see a coffee cup, think of the Sumerian who used a wheel in making round pots. When you look at a clock, think of the person who figured out the plan to have sixty minutes in an hour.

These statues of the Sumerians remind us of their many contributions to our civilization.

If you read about astronomers studying a supernova star, remember the Sumerian who made a record of one 6,000 years ago. If you hear of farmers worrying about water for their crops, remember the Sumerians who struggled to develop irrigation systems for their crops. If you read the story of Noah and the Ark, remember the Sumerian stories and the fact that Abraham was said to have come from the city of Ur, though probably at a time later than the Sumerians.

We have learned much from the Sumerians, yet are very different from them. We are free from slavery. We do not have harsh punishments from the law or in the schools. We do not have to worry much about invasion from a neighboring city or attacks from wild animals. We know much more about our world and have gained much from the other civilizations that have made gifts to us.

The legacy of the Sumerians includes their gifts of writing, counting, and learning to live together. But it is only within the last hundred years that our archaeologists have uncovered the beautiful masterpieces of art and literature that the Sumerians had created and that had been forgotten for so long. We should be grateful to those who have gone before us and taught us to tame animals, to plant crops, and to live in cities—in other words, those who began civilization.

Glossary

A-bar-gi Name of a person whose cylinder seal was found by Woolley in the tombs at Ur

Akkadian Empire Founded by Sargon I, the Akkadians conquered the Sumerian city-states and created an empire that secured trade routes to Egypt, Lebanon, and India. It lasted from about 2334 B.C. to 2193 B.C.

An A god who was lord of the sky and patron god of Uruk

Archaeologists Scientists who study the life and culture of ancient peoples

Artifact Any object made by humans.

Assyrian Empire Later than the Sumerians, this empire in the seventh century B.C. stretched from India to Egypt and Asia Minor. The Assyrians preserved many of the Sumerian stories in their libraries of clay tablets.

Babylonian Empire Also later than the Sumerians, the Babylonians occupied the Sumerian territory from about 2700 to 538 B.C. and preserved and borrowed much of the Sumerian civilization.

Cleft A space or opening, such as in a rock, because of splitting

Cuneiform The wedge-shaped script used by the Sumerians, Akkadians, Assyrians, Babylonians, and Persians

Cylinder seal Small cylinder that was used on clay to mark possessions or as a signature by the owner of the seal. A hole was bored through the cylinder lengthwise so that it could be worn around the neck on a string.

Dumuzi A god associated with vegetation, flocks, and cattle

Egyptian Empire Ancient empire in Africa along the Nile River

Elamite tribes A group of people who conquered the Sumerian cities

Enki A god who was lord of the earth and of the fresh water of the rivers and wells

Enkidu The uncivilized man in the Epic of Gilgamesh who becomes the companion of the king, angers the gods, and dies

Enlil A god who is lord of the air and patron god of Nippur. He created the world and chose the rulers of Sumer and Akkad.

Gilgamesh The central character in the Epic of Gilgamesh. King of Uruk, he sought immortality but failed to find it.

Inanna A goddess of fertility who was responsible for the productivity of nature and humans

Lagash An important city-state that fought against other city-states. Gudea ruled here. Many statues of this ruler have survived.

Nippur A city-state that was the center of worship of Enlil, the chief deity of the Sumerians.

Persian Empire Later than the Sumerians, the Persians occupied the territory of Sumer from 539 B.C. until 331 B.C., when they were conquered by Alexander the Great. They helped in the discovery of the Sumerians through their inscriptions in cuneiform such as the tri-lingual monument at the Behistun rock.

Sargon Founder of the Akkadian Empire

Shub-ad Name of the woman discovered by Woolley in the tombs of Ur

Silt Fertile soil deposited by a river

Sledge chariot Vehicle found in the tombs of Ur. It was made of wood and was drawn by oxen.

Ur An important city-state that is the site of the discovery of the Royal Tombs by Woolley. Ur prospered during several periods of Sumerian power. One of the best preserved of the Mesopotamian ziggurats is at this location.

Ur-Nammu Founder of the third dynasty of Ur. This king's decisions in controversies were collected.

Uruk A city-state that was a great religious center.

Urukagina A king of Lagash who boasted of his justice

Ziggurat A temple tower with terraces so that each floor is slightly smaller than the one below it

Zi-u-sudra The Sumerian name for the man in the Epic of Gilgamesh who was instructed by the gods to build a big boat to escape a great flood that would destroy the earth

For Further Reading

Chimera, Edward. *They Wrote on Clay: The Babylonian Tablets Speak Today.* Edited by George C. Cameron. Chicago: The University of Chicago Press, 1986.

Cottrell, Leonard. *Lost Civilizations.* New York: Franklin Watts, 1974.

Editors of Time-Life Books. *The Age of God-Kings: Time Frame 3000–1500 B.C.* Alexandria, VA: Time-Life Books, 1987.

Hauptly, Denis J. *The Journey from the Past: A History of the Western World.* New York: Atheneum, 1983.

Lambert, David. *Ancient Peoples.* New York: Bookwright Press, 1987.

Lloyd, Seton. *The Art of the Ancient Near East.* New York: Frederick Praeger, 1961.

Stuart, Gene S. *Secrets from the Past.* Washington, DC: National Geographic, 1979.

Woolley, C. Leonard. "Introduction" in *Discovering the Royal Tombs at Ur.* Edited by Shirley Glubok. New York: Macmillan, 1969.

Index

A-bar-gi, 22, 23
Abraham, 56
Agriculture, development of,
   27, 28–29, 31, 32, 53
Akkad, 41
Akkadians, 35–37
Archaeological discoveries,
   11–12, 14, 16–25, 26, 56
Art and art objects, Sumerian,
   17, 20, 23, 26
Assyrian language, 12
Astronomy, 51, 56

Babylon, 39
Babylonian language, 12
Behistun monument, 11–
   12

Calendar, development of,
   30
City-states, 14, 16–18, 26,
   28, 35, 37, 38–52, 56
Class structure, 48
Cuneiform script, 12, 14
Cylinder seals, 22, 52

Darius I, Persian emperor,
   12

Education, 50
Elamites, 37
Enkidu, 43–44
Epic of Gilgamesh, 35, 43–44

Euphrates River, 14, 16

Family life, 49–50

Gilgamesh, Sumerian king, 25, 35, 43–44
Glacial periods, 27
Government, 28, 43, 44–49
Grave robbers, 19

Hamoudi, ibn Abrahim, 18
Hincks, Edward, 14

Iraq, 14, 25, 27

Kurdish people, 11

Lagash, city-state, 38, 49
Literature and writing, 26, 32–35, 43–44, 53, 56

Mass burials, 20–25
Mathematics
    development of, 31–32, 35, 53
Metal, use of, 28
Mud brick construction, 14, 19
Music, 20, 26

Nippur, city-state, 41, 49

Noah and the ark, story of, 26, 56

Pottery, development of, 28, 30, 53

Rawlinson, Henry Creswicke, 12
Reed huts, 25
Religion, role of, 39–46

Sails, use of, 30–31
Scribes, 33, 50, 52
Shanidar Cave, Iraq, 27
Shub-ad, 23
Slavery, 48–49
Sumerian civilization:
    city-states, 14, 16–18, 26, 28, 35, 37, 38–52
    discovery of, 11–26
    legacy of, 53–56
    religion, role of, 39–46
    rise and fall of, 27–37
Sumerian Standard, 18

Tells, 26
Tombs, excavation of, 18–25
Tools, development of, 28

Ur, city-state, 16–18, 26, 37, 56

Ur-Nammu, 49
Uruk, city-state, 43
Urukagina, 49

Warfare, 35, 46–47
Wheel, invention of, 30, 53

Wooley, Leonard, 16–25
Writing and literature, 26, 32–35, 43–44, 53, 56

Ziggurats, 39, 46
Zi-u-sudra, 44

About The Author

Leila Merrell Foster is a lawyer, a United Methodist minister, and a clinical psychologist. She lives in Evanston, Illinois. Dr. Foster has traveled in the Near East and visited Iraq, the territory in which the Sumerians lived. She has studied Biblical archaeology. Her B.S., J.D., and Ph.D. degrees are from Northwestern University, and her Master of Divinity degree is from Garrett Theological Seminary.